JUV   3/14

977.6   14 Day

EXPLORING THE STATES

Minnesota

THE NORTH STAR STATE

by Amy Rechner

BELLWET━━   ━━OLIS, MN

Note to Librarians, Teachers, and Parents:

Blastoff! Readers are carefully developed by literacy experts and combine standards-based content with developmentally appropriate text.

Level 1 provides the most support through repetition of high-frequency words, light text, predictable sentence patterns, and strong visual support.

Level 2 offers early readers a bit more challenge through varied simple sentences, increased text load, and less repetition of high-frequency words.

Level 3 advances early-fluent readers toward fluency through increased text and concept load, less reliance on visuals, longer sentences, and more literary language.

Level 4 builds reading stamina by providing more text per page, increased use of punctuation, greater variation in sentence patterns, and increasingly challenging vocabulary.

Level 5 encourages children to move from "learning to read" to "reading to learn" by providing even more text, varied writing styles, and less familiar topics.

Whichever book is right for your reader, Blastoff! Readers are the perfect books to build confidence and encourage a love of reading that will last a lifetime!

This edition first published in 2014 by Bellwether Media, Inc.

No part of this publication may be reproduced in whole or in part without written permission of the publisher. For information regarding permission, write to Bellwether Media, Inc., Attention: Permissions Department, 5357 Penn Avenue South, Minneapolis, MN 55419.

Library of Congress Cataloging-in-Publication Data

Rechner, Amy.
  Minnesota / by Amy Rechner.
    pages cm. – (Blastoff! readers. Exploring the states)
  Summary: "Developed by literacy experts for students in grades three through seven, this book introduces young readers to the geography and culture of Minnesota"– Provided by publisher.
  Includes bibliographical references and index.
  ISBN 978-1-62617-022-3 (hardcover : alk. paper)
  1. Minnesota–Juvenile literature. I. Title.
  F606.3.R43 2014
  977.6–dc23
                                                                          2013004336

Printed in the United States of America, North Mankato, MN.

Table of Contents

Where Is Minnesota?

Minnesota is a tall, broad state in the Upper **Midwest**. Canada is to the north. North Dakota and South Dakota are its western neighbors. Iowa lies to the south and Wisconsin to the east. Lake Superior's waves crash along the state's northeastern corner.

Most Minnesotans live in cities. The largest **urban** area is really two cities. Minneapolis and St. Paul are separated by the Mississippi River. St. Paul is the state capital. Rochester and Duluth are other large cities.

North Dakota

South Dakota

Canada

N
W   E
S

Minnesota

Lake
Superior

Duluth

Wisconsin

Minneapolis ⭑ St. Paul

Mississippi River

Rochester

Iowa

History

Groups of people first came to Minnesota 10,000 years ago. Their **descendants** became known as the Dakota. Europeans arrived in the 1600s. Starting in the 1830s, white settlers started pouring in to farm and harvest lumber. **Native** Americans were forced off the land. In 1858, Minnesota became a U.S. state.

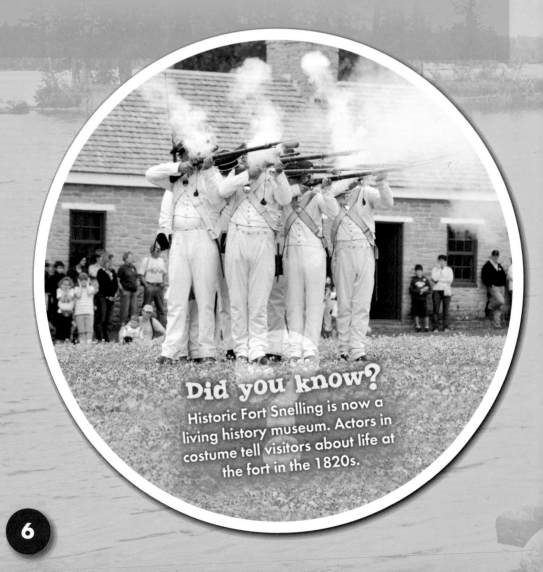

Did you know?

Historic Fort Snelling is now a living history museum. Actors in costume tell visitors about life at the fort in the 1820s.

Minnesota Timeline!

1659: Two Frenchmen are the first Europeans to reach present-day Minnesota. Fur traders soon follow.

1670s: The Ojibwe tribe moves in from the east. The Dakota and Ojibwe fight for control of the land.

1825: Fort Snelling opens. It houses both soldiers and an Indian Agency. The Agency controls trading with Ojibwe and Dakota leaders.

1858: Minnesota becomes the thirty-second state.

1862: The Dakota start the U.S.-Dakota War over broken land treaties. Almost the whole tribe is forced out of Minnesota.

1876: Bank robber Jesse James and his gang fail in their attempt to rob the First National Bank of Northfield.

1889: Dr. Charles Mayo and his brother help start the world-famous Mayo Clinic.

1998: Former professional wrestler Jesse Ventura is elected Governor of Minnesota.

U.S.-Dakota War

Dr. Charles Mayo

Jesse Ventura

The Land

Minnesota is known as the Land of 10,000 Lakes. In fact, there are more than 15,000! The lakes were carved out by **glaciers**. The largest are Red Lake and Mille Lacs Lake. Hundreds of rivers wind through the state, including the Minnesota, Mississippi, and St. Croix.

Western Minnesota used to be a tallgrass **prairie**. Now it is mostly farmland. Forests cover the northern part of the state. Minnesota's cold, snowy winters arrive early. Summers are pleasantly warm in the north. They can be hot and **humid** in the south.

St. Croix River

Minnesota's Climate

average °F

spring
Low: 32°
High: 53°

summer
Low: 56°
High: 78°

fall
Low: 34°
High: 53°

winter
Low: 4°
High: 22°

! fun fact

International Falls has earned the nickname "Icebox of the Nation." The town's lowest recorded temperature is -55 degrees Fahrenheit (-48 degrees Celsius).

The Mississippi River

The Mississippi River begins at Lake Itasca in northern Minnesota. Visitors to Lake Itasca State Park can walk across the famous river's **headwaters**. The river flows through wetlands and forests before passing through cities and **dams**.

Did **you** know?
The Mississippi River stretches from Lake Itasca to the Gulf of Mexico. That's more than 2,300 miles (3,700 kilometers)!

Mississippi River headwaters

The Mississippi gains speed as it approaches Minneapolis-St. Paul. The riverbanks grow taller. Just south of St. Paul, it meets with the Minnesota River in a deep valley. The river valley deepens further as the Mississippi joins the St. Croix River at the state's eastern border. Towering sandstone cliffs line the rushing water all the way to Iowa.

Wildlife

thirteen-lined ground squirrel

The vast forests of Minnesota are home to animals big and small. Moose, black bears, and timber wolves roam among the trees. Skunks and muskrats scurry underfoot. Otters and beavers make homes near the state's many rivers. Walleye and bass swim in the lakes while geese and loons paddle at the surface.

loon

beaver

timber wolf

Minnesota's wooded areas are filled with fir trees in the north. Oak, elm, and ash trees stand in forests and backyards in the southeast. Southwestern Minnesota has fewer trees. Asters, goldenrods, and other prairie wildflowers bloom there.

Landmarks

The Boundary Waters Canoe Area is one of the largest wild areas in the country. Outdoor adventurers travel here for canoeing and **backpacking** trips. Nature lovers can also enjoy breathtaking views on the North Shore **Scenic** Drive. This route follows the Lake Superior shore from Duluth to Grand Portage. Hikers stop off at Gooseberry Falls and Split Rock Lighthouse.

Bloomington's Mall of America is the nation's biggest mall. It has more than 500 stores and restaurants. It also has an indoor theme park with rollercoaster and water rides.

Boundary Waters Canoe Area

Mall of America

Split Rock Lighthouse

Twin Cities

Did you know?

Charles Schulz, the creator of the *Peanuts* comic strip, grew up in St. Paul. Statues of Charlie Brown, Snoopy, and all their friends decorate downtown St. Paul.

Minneapolis and St. Paul share the Twin Cities nickname. However, the two are very different. St. Paul is known for its historic neighborhoods and buildings. The Minnesota State **Capitol** sits proudly atop a hill overlooking the Minnesota History Museum and downtown St. Paul.

Minneapolis

Minnesota State Capitol

Walker Art Center

Minneapolis is larger and has an impressive chain of lakes running through it. It also has more modern buildings. Downtown skyscrapers are linked by **skyways** so visitors can avoid cold weather. The Walker Art Center displays works of art and sculpture, including a giant cherry on a spoon. Minneapolis is also known for its many theater companies that draw actors from all over the country.

Working

fun fact !

Scotch tape and Post-it Notes were invented in Minnesota at the 3M Company. Both the Jolly Green Giant and the Pillsbury Doughboy also come from Minnesota.

Minnesota was built by **immigrants** who worked on farms, in mines, and in **lumber camps**. Farms today produce wheat, corn, soybeans, livestock, and turkeys. Southern Minnesota's rich soil is perfect for growing vegetables. Taconite, granite, and clay are mined in northern Minnesota.

Minnesota's busy factories make computers, medical products, food products, and more. Most of the state's workers have **service jobs**. One of the biggest companies is the Target Corporation. It heads the national chain of stores with the bulls-eye logo. Many of Minnesota's service workers also work in **tourism** and health care.

Where People Work in Minnesota

manufacturing
10%

farming and
natural resources
3%

government
12%

services
75%

Playing

Minnesota's natural beauty lures people outside in all seasons. The many lakes and rivers offer canoeing, swimming, boating, and fishing. Winter brings ice hockey, cross-country skiing, and **snowmobiling**. Ice fishing shacks appear on frozen lakes. **Hardy** fishers try to snag a walleye through a hole in the ice. Some shacks are cozy shelters with sofas and TVs.

Minnesotans are passionate about team sports. They root for the Twins baseball team and Minnesota Wild hockey team. The Vikings also bring excitement to the state's football fans.

fun fact

Brainerd hosts an Ice Fishing Extravaganza every winter. More than 12,000 Minnesotans bundle up for this contest on frozen Gull Lake.

Brainerd Ice Fishing Extravaganza

Minnesota Twins game

Creamy Wild Rice Soup

Ingredients:

- 1/3 cup onion, finely chopped
- 6 tablespoons butter
- 1/2 cup flour
- 3 cups chicken broth
- 2 cups cooked wild rice
- 1/2 cup grated carrots
- 1 cup chicken breast strips, cooked and chopped
- 3 tablespoons slivered almonds
- 1/2 teaspoon salt
- 1 cup half & half

Directions:

1. In large saucepan, sauté onions in butter.

2. Add flour, stirring constantly until bubbly. Gradually stir in broth.

3. Add wild rice, carrots, chicken, almonds, and salt. Simmer 5 minutes.

4. Add half & half. Heat through.

   Makes 6 servings.

spam

lutefisk

Minnesota is famous for walleye, wild rice, and large apple and berry harvests. The state's food also reflects the heritage of its people. **Scandinavian** settlers relied on a dried whitefish called lutefisk for food in winter. Lutefisk is still served across Minnesota during the holiday season.

New Ulm is known for its **traditional** German food. Middle Eastern dishes reflect Mankato's large Lebanese community. The town of Hibbing treasures the porketta. This shredded pork roast sandwich was originally eaten by Italian miners. Immigrants from Southeast Asia brought the flavors of Vietnam, Thailand, and Laos to the Twin Cities.

Festivals

Minnesota has fun for all seasons. The St. Paul Winter Carnival features parades, snow and ice sculptures, and sometimes an ice palace. In summer, the Minneapolis Aquatennial showcases summer sports and concerts around the city's lakes.

Northfield honors its history with Defeat of Jesse James Days. Actors play out the failed robbery, including a getaway on horseback. Everyone looks forward to the State Fair in St. Paul. Rides, games, and concerts fill the day. Farmers display their prize livestock and produce. The State Fair is famous for corn dogs and many other foods on a stick.

Minnesota State Fair

St. Paul Winter Carnival Ice Palace

Did you know?

The small town of Whalan is only a couple blocks long. During its Stand Still Parade, floats and cars park down the center of the street. The paradegoers are the ones who move!

Minnesota's deep forests once attracted lumberjacks and tall tales. The most famous story tells of Paul Bunyan and Babe, his blue ox. According to **folklore**, Paul Bunyan is a giant lumberjack with super-human strength. One tale says he dug out Lake Superior to get water for his ox. Another says Minnesota's lakes were formed by Paul and Babe's footprints.

Minnesotans love Paul Bunyan. The town of Bemidji put up giant statues of Paul and Babe in 1937. Paul Bunyan Land in Brainerd features a talking statue of the great lumberjack. Thousands of people pay a visit to Paul and Babe each year. They take photos with the towering pair and enjoy the beauty of Minnesota's Northwoods.

Fast Facts About Minnesota

Minnesota's Flag

Minnesota's flag is royal blue. The state seal is in the center. It shows a farmer in a field and a Native American riding by on horseback. Above the image is a banner with the state motto. A wreath of lady's slippers surrounds the seal. Nineteen stars sit outside the wreath. They show that Minnesota was the nineteenth state to join the Union after the first thirteen.

State Flower
pink and white lady's slipper

State Nicknames:	North Star State
	Gopher State
	Land of 10,000 Lakes
State Motto:	*L'Etoile du Nord;*
	"The Star of the North"
Year of Statehood:	1858
Capital City:	St. Paul
Other Major Cities:	Minneapolis, Rochester, Duluth
Population:	5,303,925 (2010)
Area:	86,935 square miles
	(225,161 square kilometers);
	Minnesota is the 12th largest state.
Major Industries:	health care, tourism,
	manufacturing, mining, farming
Natural Resources:	iron ore, granite, forests, water
State Government:	134 representatives; 67 senators
Federal Government:	8 representatives; 2 senators
Electoral Votes:	10

State Bird
common loon

State Animal
walleye

Glossary

backpacking—long-distance hiking; backpackers often carry equipment for camping.

capitol—the building in which state representatives and senators meet

dams—structures that block the flow of water in a river

descendants—people who come from a common ancestor

folklore—stories, customs, and beliefs that are handed down from one generation to the next

glaciers—massive sheets of ice that cover large areas of land

hardy—able to bear harsh and changing conditions

headwaters—the starting point of a stream or river

humid—damp and sticky

immigrants—people who leave one country to live in another country

lumber camps—small communities of lumberjacks hired to chop down trees

Midwest—a region of 12 states in the north-central United States

native—originally from a specific place

prairie—a large area of level or rolling grassland

Scandinavian—from Denmark, Norway, or Sweden

scenic—providing beautiful views of the natural surroundings

service jobs—jobs that perform tasks for people or businesses

skyways—covered bridges that connect buildings in a city

snowmobiling—the sport of driving snowmobiles; snowmobiles are vehicles that move quickly over snow.

tourism—the business of providing services to travelers

traditional—relating to a custom, idea, or belief handed down from one generation to the next

urban—relating to the city

To Learn More

AT THE LIBRARY

Heinrichs, Ann. *Minnesota*. New York, N.Y.:
Children's Press, 2009.

Kennedy, Mike. *Meet the Vikings*. Chicago, Ill.:
Norwood House Press, 2011.

Wilder, Laura Ingalls. *On the Banks of Plum Creek*.
New York, N.Y.: HarperTrophy, 2004.

ON THE WEB

Learning more about Minnesota
is as easy as 1, 2, 3.

1. Go to www.factsurfer.com.

2. Enter "Minnesota" into the search box.

3. Click the "Surf" button and you will see a list of
   related Web sites.

With factsurfer.com, finding more information is just
a click away.

Index